My First Animal Library

Camels

by Mari Schuh

Bullfrog Books

Ideas for Parents and Teachers

Bullfrog Books let children practice reading informational text at the earliest reading levels. Repetition, familiar words, and photo labels support early readers.

Before Reading
- Discuss the cover photo. What does it tell them?

- Look at the picture glossary together. Read and discuss the words.

Read the Book
- "Walk" through the book and look at the photos. Let the child ask questions. Point out the photo labels.

- Read the book to the child, or have him or her read independently.

After Reading
- Prompt the child to think more. Ask: Have you ever seen a camel? Where did you see it?

Bullfrog Books are published by Jump!
5357 Penn Avenue South
Minneapolis, MN 55419
www.jumplibrary.com

Copyright © 2015 Jump! International copyright reserved in all countries. No part of this book may be reproduced in any form without written permission from the publisher.

Library of Congress Cataloging-in-Publication Data

Schuh, Mari C., 1975– author.
 Camels / by Mari Schuh.
   pages cm.—(Bullfrog books.
 My first animal library)
 Audience: Age 5.
 Audience: K to grade 3.
 Includes index.
 ISBN 978-1-62031-174-5 (hardcover)
 ISBN 978-1-62496-261-5 (ebook)
 1. Camels—Juvenile literature. I. Title.
 QL737.U54S38 2015
 599.63'62—dc23

                                2014032158

Series Editor: Wendy Dieker
Series Designer: Ellen Huber
Book Designer: Lindaanne Donohoe
Photo Researcher: Jenny Fretland VanVoorst

Photo Credits: All photos by Shutterstock except: iStock, 1, 16, 23bl; Thinkstock, cover, 3, 5, 10, 15, 23tr, 23br.

Printed in the United States of America at Corporate Graphics in North Mankato, Minnesota.

For Avery and Cami—MS

Table of Contents

Life in the Desert

A camel walks in the desert.

He looks for
food and water.

He walks for miles.

He can go without water for days.

hump

Look at his hump!
It is full of fat.
It gives him energy.

He walks on loose sand.

How?

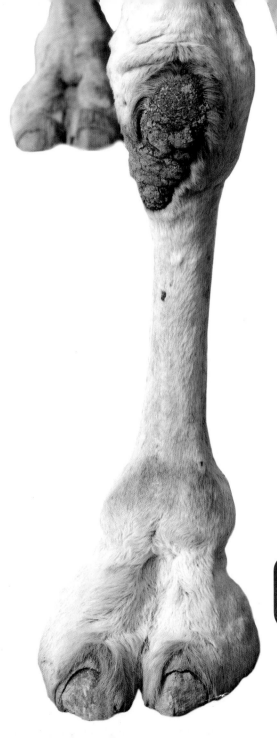

He has wide feet.

See his eyelashes?

They keep out sand.

eyelashes

12

His fur is woolly.
It protects him from
heat and cold.

fur

Oh, look!
Water!

It is an oasis.

He drinks a lot.

The camel finds food.
He eats shrubs, twigs, and thorns.

Now he is full.

He kneels down to rest.

Parts of a Camel

eyebrows
Bushy eyebrows protect a camel's eyes from blowing sand and the bright sun.

hump
Humps are full of fat. Some camels have one hump. Other camels have two humps.

nostrils
Camels can shut their nostrils to keep out sand.

feet
A camel's wide feet keep it from sinking ino the desert sand.

Picture Glossary

desert
A dry area of land where very little rain falls; deserts can be hot and cold.

thorn
A sharp point growing on a plant.

oasis
An area in a desert that has water.

woolly
Having soft, thick, and often curly hair.

Index

To Learn More

Learning more is as easy as 1, 2, 3.

1) Go to www.factsurfer.com

2) Enter "camels" into the search box.

3) Click the "Surf" button to see a list of websites.

With factsurfer.com, finding more information is just a click away.